First Book
of Flute Solos

Erstes Spiel...

...CE

...NNING

...ted

Contents : Inhalt

© 1984 by Faber Music Ltd
First published in 1984 by Faber Music Ltd
3 Queen Square London WC1N 3AU
Music drawn by Sheila Stanton
Cover design by Roslav Szaybo and Studio Gerrard
Printed in England by Caligraving Ltd

Separate flute parts are available

Preface

This collection aims to introduce players at a fairly early stage to an unusually wide range of music. All the pieces have been chosen to encourage attention to the basic technical aspects of flute-playing, and in this respect they progress throughout the book. There is special emphasis on the production of a good sound, and we cannot stress too strongly the great care this requires. At the same time we have aimed to provide music that is simply a pleasure to play; through working at these melodies the flautist should begin to develop his or her own naturally expressive style as well as a good basic technique.

The piano accompaniments should always be played lightly; the flautist should not have to strain to be heard. Short explanatory notes have been provided for each piece. Some metronome markings are included, as helpful suggestions rather than strict instructions.

JUDITH PEARCE
CHRISTOPHER GUNNING

Vorwort

Diese Sammlung möchte den Spieler bereits in ziemlich frühem Stadium mit einem ungewöhnlich weiten musikalischen Gebiet vertraut machen. Alle Stücke wurden unter dem Aspekt ausgewählt, die Aufmerksamkeit auf die grundlegenden technischen Probleme des Flötenspiels zu lenken, und sie steigern sich daher in dieser Hinsicht das ganze Album hindurch. Besonderer Wert wurde auf die Erzeugung eines guten Tones gelegt, und wir können die Sorgfalt, die diese erfordert, gar nicht genug betonen. Gleichzeitig jedoch beabsichtigten wir, Musik zu bieten, die einfach Freude macht zu spielen: durch die Arbeit an diesen Melodien soll der/die Flötist(in) damit beginnen, seinen/ihren eigenen natürlich, expressiven Stil sowie eine gute, grundlegende Technik zu entwickeln.

Die Klavierbegleitung sollte immer leicht gespielt werden; der/die Flötist(in) sollte sich nicht anstrengen müssen, um gehört zu werden. Jedem Stück wurde eine kurze erläuternde Anmerkung beigegeben. Einige Metronomangaben, die jedoch eher als hilfreiche Vorschläge denn als strikte Anweisungen gedacht sind, wurden beigefügt.

JUDITH PEARCE
CHRISTOPHER GUNNING

ÜBERSETZUNG: DOROTHEE EBERHARDT

1. WOOD SMOKE
Holzrauch

C.G./J.P.

Quite slow and plaintively (♩ =92)
Ziemlich langsam und klagend

29

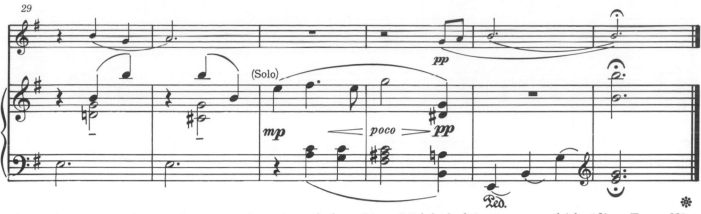

This needs a warm, steady tone. Listen to your intonation and take care over the dynamics and the slurs.	Dieses Stück bedarf eines warmen, gleichmäßigen Tones. Höre genau auf deine Intonation, und achte auf die dynamischen Bezeichnungen und die Bögen.

2. COVENTRY CAROL

Weihnachtslied aus Coventry

Traditional
(Original version, 1591)

Tongue every note clearly. Tongue and embouchure should be relaxed, not tight. Make a clear, firm sound from beginning to end. Notice the changes of time signature.

Stoße jede Note deutlich an. Zunge und Ansatz sollten locker, nicht angespannt sein. Erzeuge einen klaren, starken Ton von Anfang bis Ende. Beachte die Taktwechsel.

3. BABIOLE
Tand

J.-C. NAUDOT
(c. 1690–1762)

Keep the rhythm crisp but robust; the notes should be quite short but always full-toned.

Halte einen lebendigen, jedoch kräftigen Rhythmus ein. Die Noten sollten ziemlich kurz, aber immer mit vollem Ton gespielt werden.

4. POLISH FOLK TUNE
Polnische Volksweise

Traditional

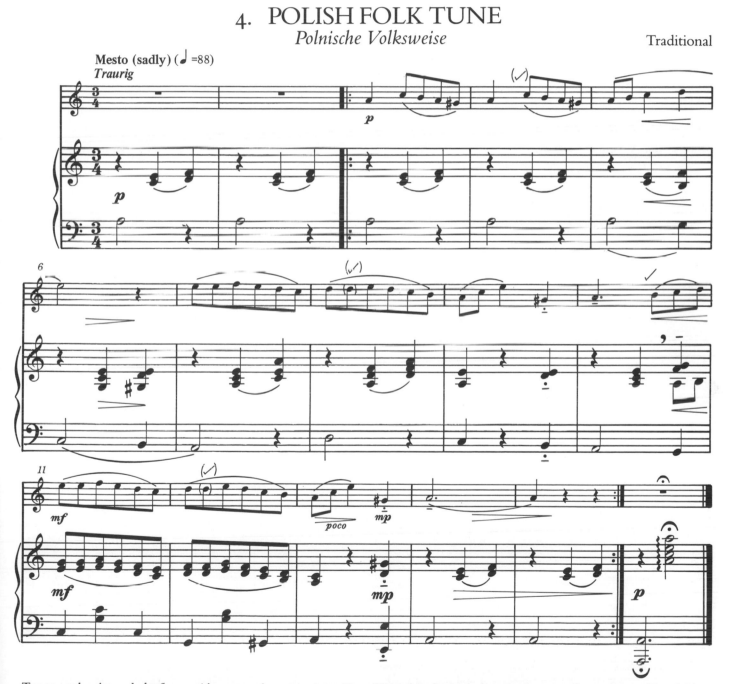

Try to make the melody flow, with a smooth, warm tone. To avoid stretching for G#, make sure that you begin with the left hand in a good position. Missing out a quaver, as marked, will allow you to breathe comfortably in bars 8 and 12.

Versuche, die Melodie mit einem sanften, warmen Ton dahinfließen zu lassen. Achte darauf, daß du zu Beginn die linke Hand in guter Grifflage hast, um das Spreizen der Finger für das Gis zu vermeiden. Wenn du, wie eingezeichnet, ein Achtel ausläßt, wirst du in den Takten 8 und 12 bequem atmen können.

5. SANDMÄNNCHEN

J. BRAHMS
(1833–1897)

At a moving speed (♩=92)
In bewegtem Tempo

This is a gentle, sleepy song. Sing through each phrase with a sweet tone, and try to produce the same sort of sound for every C#. Always be aware of the moving quavers in the piano part and make sure that you keep in time with them; be particularly careful after breaths.

Dies ist ein sanftes, verträumtes Lied. Singe mit weichem Ton durch jede Phrase und versuche, bei jedem Cis die gleiche Art von Ton hervorzubringen. Denke immer an die bewegten Achtel in der Klavierstimme und achte darauf, daß du im Takt mit ihnen spielst; sei besonders sorgsam nach dem Atemholen.

6. ELEGY
Elegie

C.G./J.P.

Descending to the very bottom notes on the flute takes a great deal of slow, gradual practice. This Elegy should help you to work at this. Always play with a warm, relaxed tone, whether pp or mf. Take care to give the second note of each pair of quavers its full length. Try not to alter the shape of the embouchure too much when you breathe; this will help you to keep a steady tone on the bottom notes.

Das Hinunterspielen zu den tiefsten Noten der Flöte bedarf vielen langsamen, stufenweisen Übens. Diese Elegie soll dir helfen, daran zu arbeiten. Spiele immer mit einem warmen, unverkrampften Ton, sei es pp oder mf. Achte darauf, daß du die zweite Note eines jeden Paares von Achtelnoten ganz aushältst. Verändere die Form deines Ansatzes möglichst nicht zu sehr wenn du einatmest: dies wird dir dabei helfen, bei den tiefsten Noten einen gleichmäßigen Ton beizubehalten.

7. POPPY
Mohn

C.G./J.P.

This piece needs even fingering and careful attention to dynamics. Play the first note of each scale passage clearly and with a slight stress.

Dieses Stück bedarf gleichmäßiger Fingerbewegungen und sorgfältiger Beachtung der dynamischen Bezeichnungen. Spiele die erste Note jeder Tonleiterpassage deutlich und mit leichter Betonung.

8. GEORDIE

Traditional

Try to make as beautiful a sound as possible, and feel the rise and fall of each phrase. Take care to breathe in the places marked.

Versuche, einen möglichst schönen Ton hervorzubringen, und fühle Steigen und Fallen einer jeden Phrase. Achte darauf, daß du an den dafür bezeichneten Stellen einatmest.

9. AIR ÉCOSSAIS

Schottische Weise

L. VAN BEETHOVEN
(1770–1827)

This folk song should have a good swinging rhythm. Keep all the quavers fairly short and give them a clear, full tone.

Dieses Volkslied sollte einen guten, schwingenden Rhythmus haben. Spiele alle Achtel ziemlich kurz, und gib ihnen einen klaren, vollen Ton.

10. DOUCE DAME
Sanfte Dame

Trouvères
(12th century)

This is an early French song, so imagine you are singing the tune. Make your sound clear but warm, with no tightness in the embouchure. Try to keep a one-in-the-bar feel, articulating the tongued notes within each phrase clearly but not explosively.

Dies ist eine altes französisches Lied; stelle dir daher vor, daß du die Melodie singst. Spiele deinen Ton klar aber warm, ohne Anspannung des Ansatzes. Versuche im Gefühl von einem Taktschlag pro Takt zu spielen, und artikuliere dabei die angestoßenen Noten jeder Phrase deutlich, aber nicht explosionsartig.

11. MOONLIGHT
Mondlicht

Traditional
(Armenian Peasant Song)

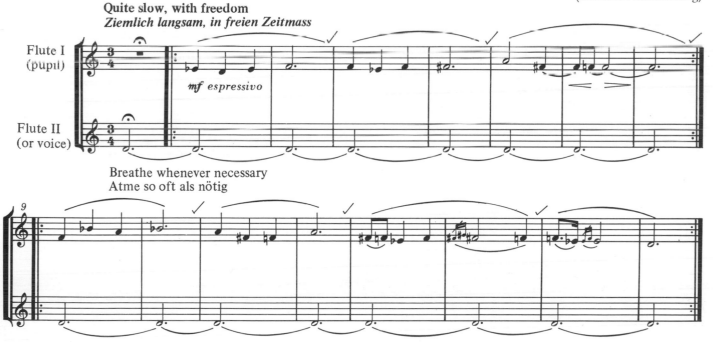

This peasant song has been barred in 3/4 to make it easier to read, but it should be played quite freely. Don't rush the breaths, and imagine that you are singing with a good, firm tone.

Dieses Bauernlied wurde durch Taktstriche in 3/4 Takte unterteilt, um das Lesen einfacher zu machen; es sollte jedoch ziemlich frei gespielt werden. Atme nicht zu hastig ein und stelle dir vor, du sängest mit einem guten, kräftigen Ton.

14

12. ECHOES
Echos

C.G./J.P.

This piece is a conversation between the flute and the piano; try to match the piano in both tone and intonation. The fingering needs careful attention.

Dieses Stück ist ein Gespräch zwischen der Flöte und dem Klavier. Versuche, dich dem Klavier in Ton und Intonation anzupassen. Der Fingersatz bedarf sorgfältiger Beachtung.

13. VIVACE IN C

F.J. HAYDN
(1732–1809)

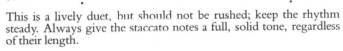

This is a lively duet, but should not be rushed; keep the rhythm steady. Always give the staccato notes a full, solid tone, regardless of their length.

Dies ist ein lebhaftes Duett, das jedoch nicht hastig gespielt werden sollte; halte einen gleichmäßigen Rhythmus ein. Gib den Stakkatonoten immer einen kräftigen, vollen Ton, ungeachtet ihrer Länge.

14. GRANDMOTHER'S FOOTSTEPS

Großmutters Fußstapfen

C.G./J.P.

This should be played delicately. Listen to the piano part and keep perfectly in time with it. Place staccato notes carefully, with real tone; don't allow them to become breathy. Give a warm, smooth tone to the short, slurred phrases.

Dieses Stück sollte feinfühlig gespielt werden. Höre der Klavierstimme zu und spiele genau im Takt mit ihr. Spiele die Stakkatonoten sorgfältig, mit richtigem Ton: lasse keinen Hauchlaut sich einschleichen. Gib den kurzen, gebundenen Phrasen einen warmen, weichen Ton.

15. PRELUDE
Präludium

F.F. CHOPIN
(1810–1849)

This is an arrangement of a well-known and much loved piece for solo piano, so the sounds of flute and piano must blend together.

Dies ist ein Arrangement eines sehr bekannten und beliebten Stückes für Soloklavier. Die Klänge von Flöte und Klavier müssen daher harmonisch miteinander verschmelzen.

16. TURKISH MARCH

Türkischer Marsch

C.M. VON WEBER
(1786-1826)

You may need to breathe after every 2 bars, but think in 4-bar phrases if you can. Try to make the rhythm bounce.

Vielleicht mußt du alle zwei Takte einatmen; denke jedoch, wenn möglich, in 4-taktigen Phrasen. Versuche, den Rhythmus federn zu lassen.

17. FAITH (Tro)

Vertrauen

E.H. GREIG
(1843-1907)

Tongue every note clearly but lightly. This is a song, so don't let your articulations chop the melodic line up into small fragments; instead, shape the phrases expressively so that each note moves forward to the next. Be careful to make a substantial tone in the middle register, especially on the notes C#, D and D#.

Stoße jede Note deutlich aber leicht an. Dies ist ein Lied; zersplittere daher die Melodielinie mit deiner Artikulation nicht in kleine Bruchstücke. Gestalte diese Phrasen vielmehr mit Ausdruck, so daß jede Note weiter zur nächsten vorwärtsdrängt. Achte darauf, daß du im mittleren Register einen kräftigen Ton erzeugst, vor allem bei den Noten Cis, D und Dis.

18. THE BUGLE WALTZ

Der Jagdhornwalzer

Traditional

Try to get a good 'Waltz' feeling; stress the 1st beats and lighten the 2nd quaver of each group of 2 slurred quavers. For intervals larger than a tone, make sure your fingering is clean and accurate, otherwise 'extra' notes may creep in.

Versuche, ein gutes Walzergefühl zu erreichen; betone die jeweils ersten Taktschläge, und spiele das zweite Achtel einer jeden Gruppe von zwei gebundenen Achteln nur leicht. Achte bei Intervallen, die größer sind als ein Ganzton, darauf, daß die Fingerbewegungen sauber und genau sind, da sich sonst zusätzliche Noten einschleichen könnten.

19. DREAM DANCER
Traumtänzer

Traditional

This piece needs to "glide" along, with a beautiful legato tone. When the first melody is repeated an octave higher (from bar 5), keep it smooth and light; do not tighten the embouchure, but think of *very* slightly "lifting" the sound. Lean gently on the first beat of each bar to give a lilting feeling. The grace notes are very quick ones (accaciaturas); touch them lightly, as close as possible to the melody note they precede.

N.B.: A tight embouchure will produce a tight, thin tone.

Dieses Stück muß mit einem schönen Legatoton "dahingleiten". Spiele die erste Melodie, wenn sie ab Takt 5 eine Oktave höher wiederholt wird, flüssig und leicht. Verwende keinen zu gespannten Ansatz, denke dir jedoch, daß du den Ton *sehr* leicht "anhebst". Lehne dich sanft an den ersten Taktschlag eines jeden Taktes an, um ein rhythmisches Gefühl zu erzeugen. Die Verzierungen sind sehr kurz (Vorschläge); spiele sie leicht und so nahe wie möglich bei der Melodienote, der sie vorangehen.

N.B.: Ein angespannter Lippenansatz erzeugt einen gepressten, dünnen Ton.

20. THE HEN
Die Henne

J. BRAHMS
(1833-1897)

This is a sunny tune; make the staccato notes light and clear, and watch out carefully for the different slurs and articulations, as well as the dynamic contrasts.

Dies ist ein fröhliches Lied. Spiele die Stakkatonoten leicht und deutlich, und achte sorgfältig auf die verschiedenen Bögen und Artikulationsarten, und auf die dynamischen Kontraste.

21. PRELUDE
Präludium

A.N. SCRIABIN
(1872-1915)

Once you are sure of the accidentals, this piece will give you an opportunity to improve your sound. Listen to yourself as you play, to hear if you are making as good and round a tone as possible. This is especially important at quiet dynamics.
N.B.: Be especially fussy about the sound you make on C#.

Wenn du die Versetzungszeichen erst einmal gut kennst, wird dir dieses Stück die Gelegenheit geben, deinen Ton zu verbessern. Höre dir selber zu wenn du spielst, um herauszufinden, ob du einen möglichst guten und runden Ton erzeugst. Dies ist besonders bei den Bezeichnungen für leises Spielen wichtig.
N.B.: Sei besonders penibel hinsichtlich des Tones, den du beim Cis hervorbringst.

22. WIEDERSEHN

F.P. SCHUBERT
(1797–1828)

Make a warm, fluent sound which will carry smoothly through every interval, no matter whether it's a 3rd or a 7th.

Erzeuge einen warmen, flüssigen Ton, der glatt durch jedes Intervall trägt, sei dies eine Terz oder eine Septime.

23. MARIONETTES ESPAGNOLES

Spanische Marionetten

C.A. CUI
(1835-1918)

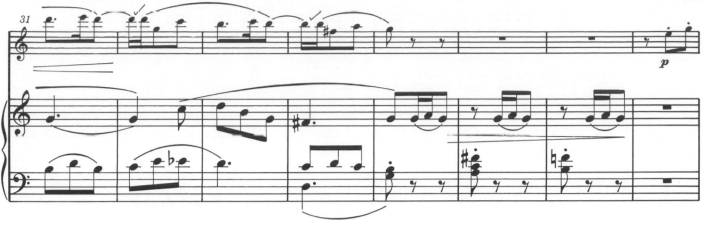

Articulate each staccato note, however short, clearly and with real substance of tone. The middle section (bars 21-37) needs smoothly phrased lines. Be sure to bring off the tied notes accurately.

Artikuliere jede noch so kurze Stakkatonote deutlich und mit wirklich kräftigem Ton. Der mittlere Abschnitt (Takte 21-37) bedarf sanft phrasierter Linien. Sei sicher, daß du die angebundenen Noten genau spielst.

24. THE SONG MY LUTE ONCE LOVED

Das Lied, das meine Laute einst liebte

J. DOWLAND
(1563-1626)

This melody is simple but beautiful. Play at an even dynamic all the way through, but bring out the natural rise and fall of each phrase. Make a clear, warm sound.

Diese Melodie ist einfach aber schön. Spiele durchweg mit gleicher Lautstärke, aber bringe das natürliche Steigen und Fallen einer jeden Phrase zum Ausdruck. Erzeuge einen deutlichen, warmen Ton.

25. CIRCUS TURN
Zirkusnummer

C.G./J.P.

This piece takes its sense of fun and good humour from Kabalevsky's *Clowns* for solo piano. The music is rather comical, so try to catch this spirit, as well as playing good, clear rhythms. The piece will also give you practise in chromatic fingerings, particularly around the break; remember that middle E♭ does *not* use the l.h. index finger and that your hands must be in good positions.

Dieses Stück hat seinen Sinn für Spaß und gute Laune von Kabalewskijs *Clowns* für Soloklavier. Die Musik ist ziemlich lustig; bemühe dich daher, diese Stimmung einzufangen und gleichzeitig gute, klare Rhythmen zu spielen. Das Stück gibt dir auch Übung in chromatischen Fingersätzen, besonders um den Registerwechsel herum. Vergiß nicht, daß für das mittlere Es *nicht* der Zeigefinger der linken Hand verwendet wird, und daß deine Hände in guter Griffposition sein müssen.

26. CHICKEN CHOWDER
Hühnereintopf

I.M. GIBLIN

This is an American Rag, so emphasize the syncopations (ie: the off-beats) and try to make the whole piece sound witty.

Dies ist ein amerikanischer Ragtime; betone daher die synkopierten Noten (d.h. die Offbeats), und versuche so zu spielen, daß das ganze Stück witzig klingt.

27. GNOSSIENNE

E. SATIE
(1866–1925)

Avec une légere intimité

Sans orgueil

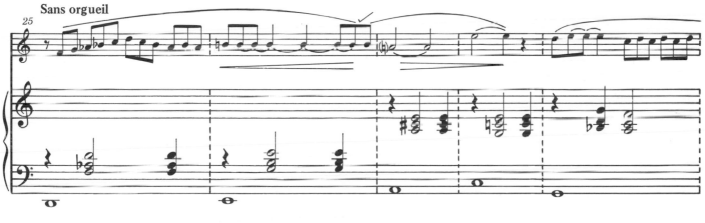

pp

In its original form this piece has no bar-lines, so the effect should be one of continuous movement. First of all, read carefully through the flute part, paying particular attention to the triplets (these are less complicated than they look) and the various groups of tied notes. Remember to check hand positions before you begin, and then practise each phrase separately, at a slow tempo. Make a clear, warm tone, without overdoing the crescendos and diminuendos.

Dieses Stück hat in seiner ursprünglichen Form keine Takt-striche, d.h. der Effekt sollte der einer ununterbrochenen Bewegung sein. Lies die Flötenstimme zunächst sorgfältig durch, und beachte hierbei besonders die Triolen (sie sind weniger kompliziert als sie aussehen) und die verschiedenen Gruppen angebundener Noten. Vergiß nicht, die Griffpositionen zu überprüfen bevor du beginnst, und übe dann jede Phrase gesondert, in langsamem Tempo. Erzeuge einen klaren, warmen Ton, ohne die Crescendi und Decrescendi zu über-treiben.

First Book
of Flute Solos

Erstes Spielbuch für
Flöte und Klavier

edited and arranged by

JUDITH PEARCE

and

CHRISTOPHER GUNNING

Faber Music Limited

London

© 1984 by Faber Music Ltd
First published in 1984 by Faber Music Ltd
3 Queen Square London WC1N 3AU
Music drawn by Sheila Stanton
Cover design by Roslav Szaybo and Studio Gerrard
Printed in England by Caligraving Ltd

Contents : Inhalt

Preface

This collection aims to introduce players at a fairly early stage to an unusually wide range of music. All the pieces have been chosen to encourage attention to the basic technical aspects of flute-playing, and in this respect they progress throughout the book. There is special emphasis on the production of a good sound, and we cannot stress too strongly the great care this requires. At the same time we have aimed to provide music that is simply a pleasure to play; through working at these melodies the flautist should begin to develop his or her own naturally expressive style as well as a good basic technique.

The piano accompaniments should always be played lightly; the flautist should not have to strain to be heard. Short explanatory notes have been provided for each piece. Some metronome markings are included, as helpful suggestions rather than strict instructions.

JUDITH PEARCE
CHRISTOPHER GUNNING

Vorwort

Diese Sammlung möchte den Spieler bereits in ziemlich frühem Stadium mit einem ungewöhnlich weiten musikalischen Gebiet vertraut machen. Alle Stücke wurden unter dem Aspekt ausgewählt, die Aufmerksamkeit auf die grundlegenden technischen Probleme des Flötenspiels zu lenken, und sie steigern sich daher in dieser Hinsicht das ganze Album hindurch. Besonderer Wert wurde auf die Erzeugung eines guten Tones gelegt, und wir können die Sorgfalt, die diese erfordert, gar nicht genug betonen. Gleichzeitig jedoch beabsichtigten wir, Musik zu bieten, die einfach Freude macht zu spielen: durch die Arbeit an diesen Melodien soll der/die Flötist(in) damit beginnen, seinen/ihren eigenen natürlich, expressiven Stil sowie eine gute, grundlegende Technik zu entwickeln.

Die Klavierbegleitung sollte immer leicht gespielt werden; der/die Flötist(in) sollte sich nicht anstrengen müssen, um gehört zu werden. Jedem Stück wurde eine kurze erläuternde Anmerkung beigegeben. Einige Metronomangaben, die jedoch eher als hilfreiche Vorschläge denn als strikte Anweisungen gedacht sind, wurden beigefügt.

JUDITH PEARCE
CHRISTOPHER GUNNING

ÜBERSETZUNG: DOROTHEE EBERHARDT

1. WOOD SMOKE

Holzrauch

C.G./J.P.

Quite slow and plaintively (♩=92)
Ziemlich langsam und klagend

poco rit.

This needs a warm, steady tone. Listen to your intonation and take care over the dynamics and the slurs.

Dieses Stück bedarf eines warmen, gleichmäßigen Tones. Höre genau auf deine Intonation, und achte auf die dynamischen Bezeichnungen und die Bögen.

2. COVENTRY CAROL

Weihnachtslied aus Coventry

Traditional
(Original version, 1591)

(♩=80)

Tongue every note clearly. Tongue and embouchure should be relaxed, not tight. Make a clear, firm sound from beginning to end. Notice the changes of time signature.

Stoße jede Note deutlich an. Zunge und Ansatz sollten locker, nicht angespannt sein. Erzeuge einen klaren, starken Ton von Anfang bis Ende. Beachte die Taktwechsel.

6

3. BABIOLE
Tand

J.-C. NAUDOT
(c. 1690–1762)

Keep the rhythm crisp but robust; the notes should be quite short but always full-toned.

Halte einen lebendigen, jedoch kräftigen Rhythmus ein. Die Noten sollten ziemlich kurz, aber immer mit vollem Ton gespielt werden.

4. POLISH FOLK TUNE
Polnische Volksweise

Traditional

Try to make the melody flow, with a smooth, warm tone. To avoid stretching for G#, make sure that you begin with the left hand in a good position. Missing out a quaver, as marked, will allow you to breathe comfortably in bars 8 and 12.

Versuche, die Melodie mit einem sanften, warmen Ton dahinfließen zu lassen. Achte darauf, daß du zu Beginn die linke Hand in guter Grifflage hast, um das Spreizen der Finger für das Gis zu vermeiden. Wenn du, wie eingezeichnet, ein Achtel ausläßt, wirst du in den Takten 8 und 12 bequem atmen können.

5. SANDMÄNNCHEN

J. BRAHMS
(1833–1897)

At a moving speed (♩=92)
In bewegtem Tempo

p dolce

This is a gentle, sleepy song. Sing through each phrase with a sweet tone, and try to produce the same sort of sound for every C#. Always be aware of the moving quavers in the piano part and make sure that you keep in time with them; be particularly careful after breaths.

Dies ist ein sanftes, verträumtes Lied. Singe mit weichem Ton durch jede Phrase und versuche, bei jedem Cis die gleiche Art von Ton hervorzubringen. Denke immer an die bewegten Achtel in der Klavierstimme und achte darauf, daß du im Takt mit ihnen spielst; sei besonders sorgsam nach dem Atemholen.

6. ELEGY

Elegie

C.G./J.P.

Solemnly (♩=72)
Feierlich

mf

Descending to the very bottom notes on the flute takes a great deal of slow, gradual practice. This Elegy should help you to work at this. Always play with a warm, relaxed tone, whether pp or mf. Take care to give the second note of each pair of quavers its full length. Try not to alter the shape of the embouchure too much when you breathe; this will help you to keep a steady tone on the bottom notes.

Das Hinunterspielen zu den tiefsten Noten der Flöte bedarf vielen langsamen, stufenweisen Übens. Diese Elegie soll dir helfen, daran zu arbeiten. Spiele immer mit einem warmen, unverkrampften Ton, sei es pp oder mf. Achte darauf, daß du die zweite Note eines jeden Paares von Achtelnoten ganz aushältst. Verändere die Form deines Ansatzes möglichst nicht zu sehr wenn du einatmest: dies wird dir dabei helfen, bei den tiefsten Noten einen gleichmäßigen Ton beizubehalten.

8

7. POPPY
Mohn

C.G./J.P.

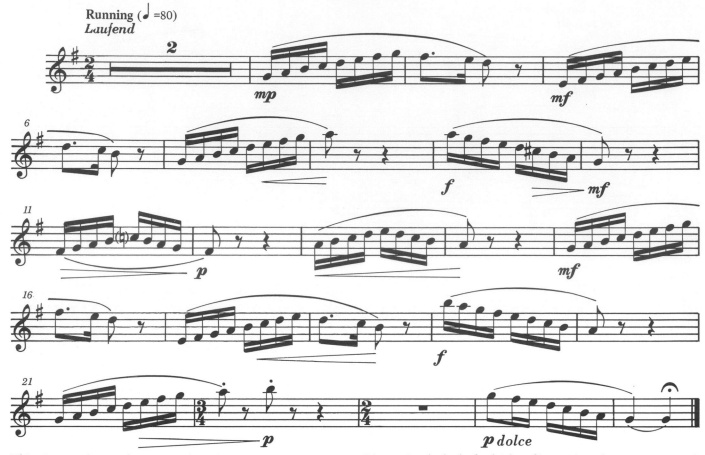

This piece needs even fingering and careful attention to dynamics. Play the first note of each scale passage clearly and with a slight stress.

Dieses Stück bedarf gleichmäßiger Fingerbewegungen und sorgfältiger Beachtung der dynamischen Bezeichnungen. Spiele die erste Note jeder Tonleiterpassage deutlich und mit leichter Betonung.

8. GEORDIE

Traditional

Try to make as beautiful a sound as possible, and feel the rise and fall of each phrase. Take care to breathe in the places marked.

Versuche, einen möglichst schönen Ton hervorzubringen, und fühle Steigen und Fallen einer jeden Phrase. Achte darauf, daß du an den dafür bezeichneten Stellen einatmest.

9. AIR ÉCOSSAIS
Schottische Weise

L. VAN BEETHOVEN
(1770-1827)

This folk song should have a good swinging rhythm. Keep all the quavers fairly short and give them a clear, full tone.

Dieses Volkslied sollte einen guten, schwingenden Rhythmus haben. Spiele alle Achtel ziemlich kurz, und gib ihnen einen klaren, vollen Ton.

10. DOUCE DAME
Sanfte Dame

Trouvères
(12th century)

This is an early French song, so imagine you are singing the tune. Make your sound clear but warm, with no tightness in the embouchure. Try to keep a one-in-the-bar feel, articulating the tongued notes within each phrase clearly but not explosively.

Dies ist eine altes französisches Lied; stelle dir daher vor, daß du die Melodie singst. Spiele deinen Ton klar aber warm, ohne Anspannung des Ansatzes. Versuche im Gefühl von einem Taktschlag pro Takt zu spielen, und artikuliere dabei die angestoßenen Noten jeder Phrase deutlich, aber nicht explosionsartig.

11. MOONLIGHT
Mondlicht

Traditional
(Armenian Peasant Song)

This peasant song has been barred in 3/4 to make it easier to read, but it should be played quite freely. Don't rush the breaths, and imagine that you are singing with a good, firm tone.

Dieses Bauernlied wurde durch Taktstriche in 3/4 Takte unterteilt, um das Lesen einfacher zu machen; es sollte jedoch ziemlich frei gespielt werden. Atme nicht zu hastig ein und stelle dir vor, du sängest mit einem guten, kräftigen Ton.

12. ECHOES
Echos

C.G./J.P.

poco rit.

This piece is a conversation between the flute and the piano; try to match the piano in both tone and intonation. The fingering needs careful attention.

Dieses Stück ist ein Gespräch zwischen der Flöte und dem Klavier. Versuche, dich dem Klavier in Ton und Intonation anzupassen. Der Fingersatz bedarf sorgfältiger Beachtung.

13. VIVACE IN C

F.J. HAYDN
(1732-1809)

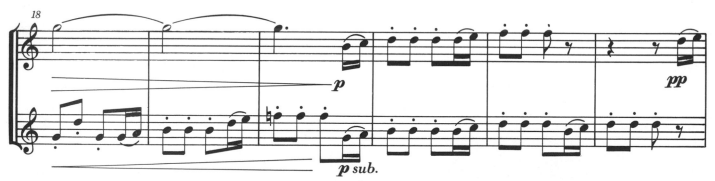

This is a lively duet, but should not be rushed; keep the rhythm steady. Always give the staccato notes a full, solid tone, regardless of their length.

Dies ist ein lebhaftes Duett, das jedoch nicht hastig gespielt werden sollte; halte einen gleichmäßigen Rhythmus ein. Gib den Stakkatonoten immer einen kräftigen, vollen Ton, ungeachtet ihrer Länge.

14. GRANDMOTHER'S FOOTSTEPS

Großmutters Fußstapfen

C.G./J.P.

This should be played delicately. Listen to the piano part and keep perfectly in time with it. Place staccato notes carefully, with real tone; don't allow them to become breathy. Give a warm, smooth tone to the short, slurred phrases.

Dieses Stück sollte feinfühlig gespielt werden. Höre der Klavierstimme zu und spiele genau im Takt mit ihr. Spiele die Stakkatonoten sorgfältig, mit richtigem Ton: lasse keinen Hauchlaut sich einschleichen. Gib den kurzen, gebundenen Phrasen einen warmen, weichen Ton.

15. PRELUDE
Präludium

F.F. CHOPIN
(1810-1849)

This is an arrangement of a well-known and much loved piece for solo piano, so the sounds of flute and piano must blend together.

Dies ist ein Arrangement eines sehr bekannten und beliebten Stückes für Soloklavier. Die Klänge von Flöte und Klavier müssen daher harmonisch miteinander verschmelzen.

16. TURKISH MARCH
Türkischer Marsch

C.M. VON WEBER
(1786-1826)

You may need to breathe after every 2 bars, but think in 4-bar phrases if you can. Try to make the rhythm bounce.

Vielleicht mußt du alle zwei Takte einatmen; denke jedoch, wenn möglich, in 4-taktigen Phrasen. Versuche, den Rhythmus federn zu lassen.

17. FAITH (Tro)
Vertrauen

E.H. GREIG
(1843-1907)

Tongue every note clearly but lightly. This is a song, so don't let your articulations chop the melodic line up into small fragments; instead, shape the phrases expressively so that each note moves forward to the next. Be careful to make a substantial tone in the middle register, especially on the notes C#, D and D#.

Stoße jede Note deutlich aber leicht an. Dies ist ein Lied; zersplittere daher die Melodielinie mit deiner Artikulation nicht in kleine Bruchstücke. Gestalte diese Phrasen vielmehr mit Ausdruck, so daß jede Note weiter zur nächsten vorwärtsdrängt. Achte darauf, daß du im mittleren Register einen kräftigen Ton erzeugst, vor allem bei den Noten Cis, D und Dis.

18. THE BUGLE WALTZ
Der Jagdhornwalzer
Traditional

With a swing (♩=144)
Mit Schwung

Try to get a good 'Waltz' feeling; stress the 1st beats and lighten the 2nd quaver of each group of 2 slurred quavers. For intervals larger than a tone, make sure your fingering is clean and accurate, otherwise 'extra' notes may creep in.

Versuche, ein gutes Walzergefühl zu erreichen; betone die jeweils ersten Taktschläge, und spiele das zweite Achtel einer jeden Gruppe von zwei gebundenen Achteln nur leicht. Achte bei Intervallen, die größer sind als ein Ganzton, darauf, daß die Fingerbewegungen sauber und genau sind, da sich sonst zusätzliche Noten einschleichen könnten.

19. DREAM DANCER
Traumtänzer
Traditional

Moderately slow (♩=92)
Mässig langsam

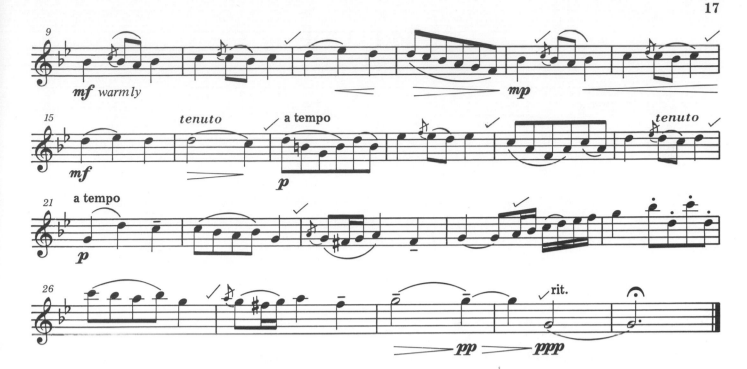

This piece needs to "glide" along, with a beautiful legato tone. When the first melody is repeated an octave higher (from bar 5), keep it smooth and light; do not tighten the embouchure, but think of *very* slightly "lifting" the sound. Lean gently on the first beat of each bar to give a lilting feeling. The grace notes are very quick ones (accaciaturas); touch them lightly, as close as possible to the melody note they precede.

N.B.: A tight embouchure will produce a tight, thin tone.

Dieses Stück muß mit einem schönen Legatoton "dahingleiten". Spiele die erste Melodie, wenn sie ab Takt 5 eine Oktave höher wiederholt wird, flüssig und leicht. Verwende keinen zu gespannten Ansatz, denke dir jedoch, daß du den Ton *sehr* leicht "anhebst". Lehne dich sanft an den ersten Taktschlag eines jeden Taktes an, um ein rhythmisches Gefühl zu erzeugen. Die Verzierungen sind sehr kurz (Vorschläge); spiele sie leicht und so nahe wie möglich bei der Melodienote, der sie vorangehen.

N.B.: Ein angespannter Lippenansatz erzeugt einen gepressten, dünnen Ton.

20. THE HEN
Die Henne

J. BRAHMS
(1833-1897)

This is a sunny tune; make the staccato notes light and clear, and watch out carefully for the different slurs and articulations, as well as the dynamic contrasts.

Dies ist ein fröhliches Lied. Spiele die Stakkatonoten leicht und deutlich, und achte sorgfältig auf die verschiedenen Bögen und Artikulationsarten, und auf die dynamischen Kontraste.

21. PRELUDE
Präludium

A.N. SCRIABIN
(1872-1915)

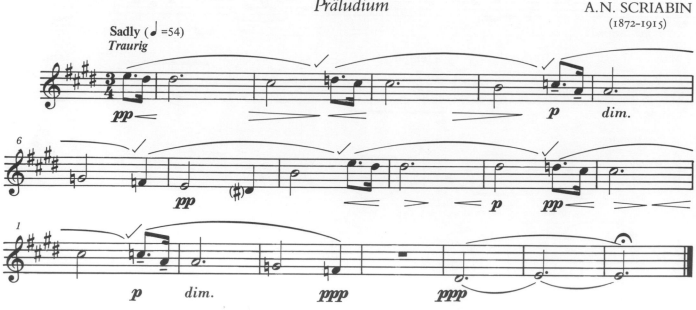

Once you are sure of the accidentals, this piece will give you an opportunity to improve your sound. Listen to yourself as you play, to hear if you are making as good and round a tone as possible. This is especially important at quiet dynamics.
N.B.: Be especially fussy about the sound you make on C#.

Wenn du die Versetzungszeichen erst einmal gut kennst, wird dir dieses Stück die Gelegenheit geben, deinen Ton zu verbessern. Höre dir selber zu wenn du spielst, um herauszufinden, ob du einen möglichst guten und runden Ton erzeugst. Dies ist besonders bei den Bezeichnungen für leises Spielen wichtig.
N.B.: Sei besonders penibel hinsichtlich des Tones, den du beim Cis hervorbringst.

22. WIEDERSEHN

F.P. SCHUBERT
(1797-1828)

Make a warm, fluent sound which will carry smoothly through every interval, no matter whether it's a 3rd or a 7th.

Erzeuge einen warmen, flüssigen Ton, der glatt durch jedes Intervall trägt, sei dies eine Terz oder eine Septime.

23. MARIONETTES ESPAGNOLES

Spanische Marionetten

C.A. CUI
(1835–1918)

Articulate each staccato note, however short, clearly and with real substance of tone. The middle section (bars 21–37) needs smoothly phrased lines. Be sure to bring off the tied notes accurately.

Artikuliere jede noch so kurze Stakkatonote deutlich und mit wirklich kräftigem Ton. Der mittlere Abschnitt (Takte 21–37) bedarf sanft phrasierter Linien. Sei sicher, daß du die angebundenen Noten genau spielst.

24. THE SONG MY LUTE ONCE LOVED

Das Lied, das meine Laute einst liebte

J. DOWLAND
(1563-1626)

This melody is simple but beautiful. Play at an even dynamic all the way through, but bring out the natural rise and fall of each phrase. Make a clear, warm sound.

Diese Melodie ist einfach aber schön. Spiele durchweg mit gleicher Lautstärke, aber bringe das natürliche Steigen und Fallen einer jeden Phrase zum Ausdruck. Erzeuge einen deutlichen, warmen Ton.

25. CIRCUS TURN

Zirkusnummer

C.G./J.P.

This piece takes its sense of fun and good humour from Kabalevsky's *Clowns* for solo piano. The music is rather comical, so try to catch this spirit, as well as playing good, clear rhythms. The piece will also give you practise in chromatic fingerings, particularly around the break; remember that middle E♭ does *not* use the l.h. index finger and that your hands must be in good positions.

Dieses Stück hat seinen Sinn für Spaß und gute Laune von Kabalewskijs *Clowns* für Soloklavier. Die Musik ist ziemlich lustig; bemühe dich daher, diese Stimmung einzufangen und gleichzeitig gute, klare Rhythmen zu spielen. Das Stück gibt dir auch Übung in chromatischen Fingersätzen, besonders um den Registerwechsel herum. Vergiß nicht, daß für das mittlere Es *nicht* der Zeigefinger der linken Hand verwendet wird, und daß deine Hände in guter Griffposition sein müssen.

26. CHICKEN CHOWDER
Hühnereintopf

I.M. GIBLIN

This is an American Rag, so emphasize the syncopations (ie: the off-beats) and try to make the whole piece sound witty.

Dies ist ein amerikanischer Ragtime; betone daher die synkopierten Noten (d.h. die Offbeats), und versuche so zu spielen, daß das ganze Stück witzig klingt.

27. GNOSSIENNE

E. SATIE
(1866-1925)

In its original form this piece has no bar-lines, so the effect should be one of continuous movement. First of all, read carefully through the flute part, paying particular attention to the triplets (these are less complicated than they look) and the various groups of tied notes. Remember to check hand positions before you begin, and then practise each phrase separately, at a slow tempo. Make a clear, warm tone, without overdoing the crescendos and diminuendos.

Dieses Stück hat in seiner ursprünglichen Form keine Takt-striche, d.h. der Effekt sollte der einer ununterbrochenen Bewegung sein. Lies die Flötenstimme zunächst sorgfältig durch, und beachte hierbei besonders die Triolen (sie sind weniger kompliziert als sie aussehen) und die verschiedenen Gruppen angebundener Noten. Vergiß nicht, die Griffposi-tionen zu überprüfen bevor du beginnst, und übe dann jede Phrase gesondert, in langsamem Tempo. Erzeuge einen klaren, warmen Ton, ohne die Crescendi und Decrescendi zu über-treiben.

Also from Faber Music:

Judith Pearce & Christopher Gunning
Second Book of Flute Solos
ISBN 0 571 50789 1

Play Solo Flute
ISBN 0 571 51006 X

The Really Easy Flute Book
ISBN 0 571 50881 2

Play Opera!
Carmen: Suite for flute & piano
ISBN 0 571 50972 X

The Magic Flute: Suite for flute & piano
ISBN 0 571 50971 1

Andrew Lloyd Webber
'Memory' from *Cats*
ISBN 0 571 50745 X

Cats selection
ISBN 0 571 50981 9

Howard Blake
'Walking in the Air' from *The Snowman*
ISBN 0 571 58018 1

The Snowman: Suite for flute and piano
ISBN 0 571 58023 8

FABER MUSIC · 3 QUEEN SQUARE LONDON

ISBN 0-571-50461

9 780571 504619